RECYCLED
science

INCREDIBLE
SNACK PACKAGE
SCIENCE

BY TAMMY ENZ

Consultant:
Marcelle A. Siegel
Associate Professor of Science Education
University of Missouri

CAPSTONE PRESS
a capstone imprint

Edge Books are published by Capstone Press,
1710 Roe Crest Drive, North Mankato, Minnesota 56003
www.mycapstone.com

Library of Congress Cataloging-in-Publication Data
Names: Enz, Tammy, author.
Title: Incredible snack package science / by Tammy Enz.
Description: North Mankato, Minnesota : Capstone Press, [2017] | Series: Edge books. Recycled
science | Audience: Ages 9-15.? | Audience: Grades 4 to 6.? | Includes bibliographical references
and index.
Identifiers: LCCN 2015045735|
ISBN 9781515708636 (library binding) |
ISBN 9781515708674 (eBook PDF)
Subjects: LCSH: Handicraft—Equipment and supplies—Juvenile literature. | Science—Study and
teaching—Juvenile literature. | Recycling (Waste, etc.)—Juvenile literature.
Classification: LCC TT160 .E585 2017 | DDC 745.5—dc23
LC record available at http://lccn.loc.gov/2015045735

Editorial Credits
Brenda Haugen, editor; Russell Griesmer, designer; Tracy Cummins, media specialist;
Kathy McColley, production specialist

Photo Credits
Capstone Studio: Karon Dubke (All images except the following); Shutterstock: JIPEN, 21, silver
tiger, 25

Design elements provided by Shutterstock: bimka, FINDEEP, fourb, Golbay, jannoon028, mexrix,
Picsfive, Sarunyu_foto, STILLFX, Your Design

Printed and bound in the USA.
009696F16

TABLE OF CONTENTS

INCREDIBLE SNACK PACKET SCIENCE

IN THE BAG

Munching a bag of snacks or tube of chips makes for a tasty break. But have you ever stopped to think of the technological marvels behind snack bags and tubes? Have you ever wondered why many have silvery insides? Maybe you've wondered if those bags and tubes could ever be used for something new. Well, pop open a snack, and eat up. Your questions are about to be answered. Sealed in these packages are all kinds of science. When repurposed, they shed light on some amazing scientific facts. Go on! Satisfy your hunger and your scientific curiosity.

BoPET

Nobody likes soggy potato chips. That's why a special kind of plastic is used for snack bags. Biaxially-oriented polyethylene terephthalate (BoPET) is finely stretched polyester lined with aluminum that makes chip bags tough. The layers also keep oily chips from leaking out. The aluminum layer keeps out oxygen that can make chips taste bad.

technological—the use of science to do technical things, such as designing complex machines

TIP:

To clean your snack bags and tubes before use, simply wipe away the oil with a paper towel. No soap is needed!

AMPLIFYING SPEAKER

Playing tunes on a smart phone or music player is great. But does your speaker let you down when you crank it up? Try amping up the sound with this project.

PUT IT TOGETHER:

STEP 1: Lay the binder clips back to back with their tabs open. Place the center of the tube between them. Use hot glue to glue the clips in place.

STEP 2: Measure and make a mark on the topside of the tube, 2 inches (5 cm) from the bottom end of the tube.

STEP 3: Use the utility knife to carefully cut a slit at this mark.

STEP 4: Using the width of your player as a guide, slowly widen the slit a little at a time. Widen the slit until you have a slot that your player will fit tightly into.

STEP 5: Loosely stuff the tissue into the open end of the tube. Make sure it doesn't bunch up.

STEP 6: Stick your player into the slot.
Face the speaker toward the open end of the can.
Sit back, and enjoy some amplified tunes!

STEP 5

REUSABLE KNOWLEDGE:

Music is caused by vibrations carried on sound waves. Waves travel through air in widening circles like ripples on water. The farther you are from a sound, the quieter it is. When you use this amp, the can captures sound waves before they spread out. The waves bounce off the can, causing an amplified sound. The tissue softens the sound to reduce echoes.

ARE YOU BEING "BUGGED" BY YOUR BAG

If you're telling a secret, stay away from chip bags. Why? Somebody may be listening! Researchers at the Massachusetts Institute of Technology (MIT) can decode bag vibrations. Using a special camera, they capture tiny bag movements. These movements are caused by vibrating sounds waves hitting the bag. You can't see the vibrations, but the camera can. Researchers can decode the vibrations into words.

amplify—increase in volume

JUMPING JACK

Would you like the power to command something to move without laying a finger on it? That power is all yours with this project. Amaze your friends with your invisible display of strength.

BRANCH OF SCIENCE: PHYSICS
CONCEPT: ELECTROSTATIC INDUCTION

YOU'LL NEED:

- Clean dry snack bag
- Ruler
- Pen
- Scissors
- Tape
- Balloon

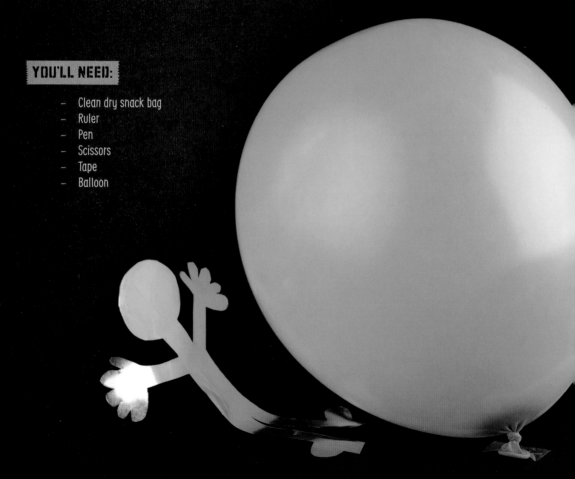

PUT IT TOGETHER:

STEP 1: Lay the bag flat. Draw the shape of half a person along one of the folded edges of the bag. Make the centerline of the person fall on the fold.

STEP 2: Cut out and unfold the person.

STEP 3: Lay the cutout on a table, silvery side down. Tape the tips of its feet to the table.

STEP 4: Flip the cutout over so the silvery side is up. Make sure the cutout still rests on the table.

STEP 5: Blow up the balloon and tie it. Hold the balloon near the cutout. What happens?

STEP 6: Rub the balloon quickly back and forth on your hair for about 10 seconds.

STEP 7: Hold the balloon over the person, and watch "Jack" jump up to grab it.

STEP 1

STEP 4

REUSABLE KNOWLEDGE:

Normally the charges in a balloon are balanced. However, when rubbing the balloon against your hair, electrons transfer. The balloon becomes negatively charged by static electricity. When held near the cutout, the balloon realigns the charges in the metal. The metal's positive charges move toward the negatively charged balloon. This realignment is called induction. So why does your hair reach out toward the balloon after rubbing it? You've given your hair a positive charge. Opposite charges attract, so your hair is attracted to the balloon.

electron—particle in an atom with a negative charge

static electricity—the buildup of an electrical charge on the surface of an object

induction—charging an object by bringing it near a charged object

UNDERWATER SPYGLASS

Looking for underwater treasure could be a lot of fun. But underwater snooping is blurry business. Pull your head out of the water. Pull out your spyglass, and clear up your water view.

BRANCH OF SCIENCE: BIOLOGY
CONCEPT: OPTICAL REFRACTION

YOU'LL NEED:

- Clean dry potato chip tube with lid
- Can opener
- Hot glue gun

SAFETY FIRST:

Have an adult help out when using hot glue, and get an adult's permission to use your spyglass in water.

PUT IT TOGETHER:

STEP 1: Use the can opener to remove the metal end of the tube.

STEP 2: Glue the lid on the other end of the can. Start by putting a bead of glue along the inside rim of the lid. Quickly put the lid on and hold it in place.

STEP 3: On the outside of the tube, place a bead of glue around the lid seam. This step makes the spyglass waterproof.

STEP 4: Take the spyglass to the lake or pool. First stick your face underwater to try to see objects beneath. What do they look like?

STEP 5: Now place the lidded end of the spyglass into the water and look into the open end. How do the objects appear now?

STEP 3

STEP 1

REUSABLE KNOWLEDGE:

As your eye absorbs light rays, it bends the rays in order to focus the image. This bending is called refraction. But water bends light rays too. When you look underwater without the spyglass, you see bent light. Your eyes can't focus this bent light. The spyglass inserts a cushion of air to help your eyes refract correctly.

refraction—a change in direction of a wave when it enters a different material

PINHOLE CAMERA

If used with film, this pinhole camera could make an image like a real camera. Both work similarly. Without film, you can still see a wacky image and learn how cameras and the human eye work.

BRANCH OF SCIENCE: **BIOLOGY**
CONCEPT: **OPTICAL INVERSION**

YOU'LL NEED:

- Clean dry potato chip tube with lid
- Ruler
- Pen
- Utility knife
- Push pin
- Waxed paper
- Scissors
- Packing tape
- Sheet of aluminum foil, about 20 inches (50 cm) long

SAFETY FIRST:

Have an adult help out when using sharp tools such as a utility knife.

PUT IT TOGETHER:

STEP 1: Measure and mark with the pen a line 2 inches (5 cm) from the bottom of the tube all around the tube.

STEP 2: Carefully cut along this line with the utility knife. You will have two sections of the tube.

STEP 3: Turn the short section of tube over. Use the push pin to make a small hole in the center of the metal end.

STEP 4: Use a pen to trace the lid on a sheet of waxed paper. Cut out this circle, and place it inside the lid.

STEP 5: Place the lid and waxed paper circle on the short section of the tube. Stack the longer section on top. Tape the pieces together.

STEP 3

STEP 2

STEP 6: Tape one end of the foil sheet to the side of the tube. Roll the foil around the tube twice. Tape it in place.

STEP 7: Wrap the foil ends over or into the tube ends.

STEP 8: Take the camera outside on a sunny day. Closing one eye, look into the open end. What do you see? Raise your hand up and down in front of the pinhole. What happens?

STEP 6

STEP 7

REUSABLE KNOWLEDGE:

Like your eye, this camera captures images upside down. Your eye sends its upside down images to your brain. Your brain automatically turns the image upright. Since the chip canister doesn't have a brain, the image remains upside down!

Your eye gathers an image through its lens and focuses it on your retina. The image is projected upside down.

retina—membrane at the back of the eye

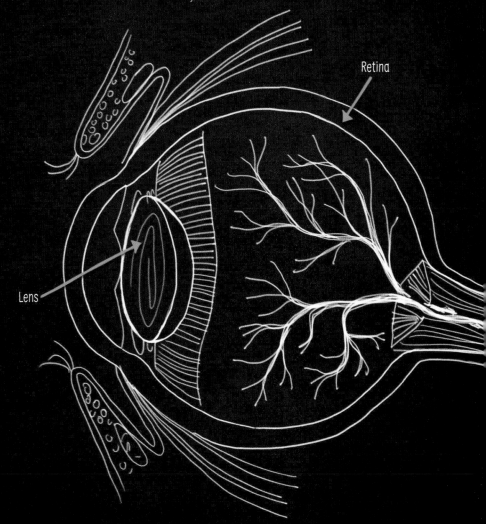

Retina

Lens

ICE CREAM MAKER

Is there a better snack than chips? You bet.
How about ice cream? Finish up your chips.
Then use the tube to create an ice cream
maker. When you do you'll learn the scientific
secret behind great ice cream.

BRANCH OF SCIENCE: CHEMISTRY
CONCEPT: MELTING POINT DEPRESSION

YOU'LL NEED:

- 4 cups (1 liter) of ice cubes
- 6 tablespoons (108 grams) rock or kosher salt
- Mixing bowl
- Spoon
- 0.5 cup (.125 L) milk
- 1 tablespoon (14 g) sugar
- 0.25 teaspoon (1.2 ml) vanilla extract

PUT IT TOGETHER:

STEP 1: Stir the ice and salt together in the bowl with the spoon. Set the bowl aside.

STEP 2: Place the milk, sugar, and vanilla in the zipper bag. Close it tightly, sealing out most of the air. Gently shake the bag to mix the ingredients.

STEP 3: Spoon ice cubes from Step 1 into the chip tube. Fill it about one quarter full.

STEP 4: Drop the zipper bag into the tube.

STEP 2

STEP 3

STEP 4

STEP 5: Carefully spoon in ice on all sides of the bag.

STEP 6: Fill the rest of the tube with ice, and put on the lid.

STEP 7: Using the towel or mitts to hold the canister, shake the tube.

STEP 8: Every two minutes, check the ice. If there is room, add more ice.

STEP 9: Continue shaking for a total of six minutes.

STEP 10: Remove the lid, pull out the bag, and open it.
Enjoy your ice cream!

REUSABLE KNOWLEDGE:

To make great ice cream you need to whip the cream mixture while freezing it. Whipping it is easy to do by shaking the chip canister. Getting it cold enough is trickier. That's where the secret ingredient, salt, comes in. Salt lowers the temperature needed to melt ice. Now more heat energy is pulled from the ice cream to melt the ice. Thus the ice cream becomes colder faster.

FAST FACT:

Normally ice melts at 32 degrees Fahrenheit (0 degrees Celsius). Adding salt can lower its melting point to as low as −6.9 degrees F (−21.6 degrees C). Putting salt on roads during the winter months keeps the ice melted even at very chilly temperatures.

STOMP ROCKET

A rocket project is always fun to make. This project relies on a snack bag's ability to hold in gas.

BRANCH OF SCIENCE: **PHYSICS**
CONCEPT: **SECOND LAW OF MOTION: FORCE=MASS X ACCELERATION**

YOU'LL NEED:

- Clean dry snack bag
- Ruler
- Scissors
- Bendable straw
- Packing tape
- Paper towel
- Water

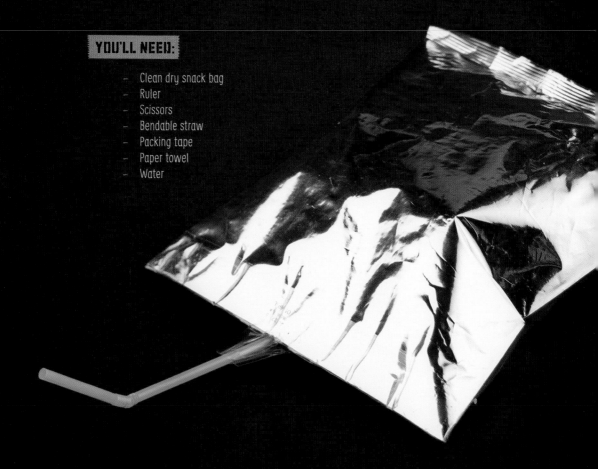

PUT IT TOGETHER:

STEP 1: Cut the top 1 inch (2.5 cm) off the opened end of the bag.

STEP 2: Stick the longer end of the straw about 2 inches (5 cm) into the bag opening. Center it in the opening.

STEP 3: Tape the straw to the inside of the bag.

STEP 4: Tape the opening of the bag shut. Make sure to tape around the straw to make it airtight.

STEP 5: Reinforce the bottom seam on the bag with more tape.

STEP 6: Blow into the straw to fill the bag. Gently squeeze it to test for air leaks. Fix any leaks with tape.

STEP 7: Moisten the towel and tear off a small piece, enough to form into a pea-sized ball.

STEP 8: Blow up the bag using the straw. Stick the ball tightly into the end of the straw.

STEP 9: Place the bag on the ground. Stomp on it to see the ball fly!

STEP 2   STEP 8

EDIBLE RAFT

Want a good idea of how much gas is in bag of chips? Two Korean college students found out in September 2014. They built a raft entirely from unopened potato chip bags. The 160 bags successfully carried them across the Han River in Seoul, South Korea.

Han River in Seoul, South Korea

REUSABLE KNOWLEDGE:

This experiment shows Newton's Second Law of Motion. This law states that acceleration is produced when a force acts on a mass. You applied a force when you smashed the bag, releasing its air. The force you applied caused the ball to accelerate or speed up. Once the ball leaves the straw, gravity works to slow it down, pulling it to the ground.

accelerate—increase speed

force—an action that changes the movement of an object

mass—the amount of matter a substance contains

SOLAR HOT DOG COOKER

Hot dogs and potato chips make great picnic food. You can have both with this project. Finish the chips. Then cook the dog. The best part is the sun does all the work.

PUT IT TOGETHER:

STEP 1: Measure and make a mark 1 inch (2.5 cm) from each end of the tube. With the tube standing, set the ruler next to it as a straightedge to connect the marks. Draw a line to connect the marks.

STEP 2: Draw another line 3 inches (7.6 cm) from this line and parallel to it.

STEP 3: Connect the ends of the lines to make a rectangle.

STEP 4: Use the utility knife to cut out the square. Save this piece for later.

STEP 5: With the lid on the tube, use the push pin to make a hole in the lid's center.

STEP 6: Remove the lid, and place it over the metal end of the tube.

STEP 7: Use the hammer and nail to punch a hole through the metal at the hole in the lid. Use the lid as a guide.

STEP 8: Stick the skewer through the bottom of the can. Leave its point sticking slightly out of the top of the can.

STEP 9: To make the base for the cooker, remove the spring from the clothespin.

STEP 3

STEP 10: Place the clothespin halves flat side down. Place them parallel to each other 4 inches (10 cm) apart.

STEP 11: Put a dab of hot glue at the spots where the spring was connected. Set the cutout from Step 4 across the clothespin halves. This forms the base for the cooker.

STEP 12: Thread a hot dog onto the skewer. Replace the lid. Make sure the skewer pokes through the lid.

STEP 13: Lay the cooker on the base.

STEP 14: Place the plastic over the opening. Tape one of the long sides to the cooker.

STEP 15: Place the cooker in a sunny place. Rotate the cooker on the base so that the hot dog faces the sun.

STEP 16: Wait 15 to 30 minutes for the hotdog to cook. Lift the plastic flap to test if it is ready. Enjoy!

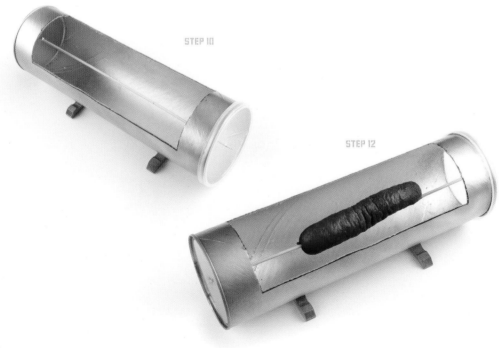

STEP 10

STEP 12

REUSABLE KNOWLEDGE:

The sun is a powerful energy source. On a sunny day, the sun supplies 100 watts of energy per 1 square foot (0.1 square meter). That's enough to light up a bright light bulb. The secret to this project is capturing and focusing that power. The metallic curved shape of the cooker does just that.

HERO'S ENGINE

A couple thousand years ago, a mathematician and inventor called Hero of Alexandria created a unique engine. It propelled itself by shooting steam out of small holes. Using a chip can, you can make a similar machine. Yours will use water and the power of hydraulic head.

BRANCH OF SCIENCE: PHYSICS
CONCEPT: HYDRAULIC HEAD

YOU'LL NEED:

- Potato chip tube
- Ruler
- Pen
- Scissors
- 2 bendable drinking straws
- Hot glue gun
- 3 feet (1 meter) string
- Pitcher of water

SAFETY FIRST:

Have an adult help you when using hot glue.

PUT IT TOGETHER:

STEP 1: Measure and make a mark 1 inch (2.5 cm) from the bottom of the can.

STEP 2: Using the tip of the scissors, punch a hole at this point. Twist the scissors point through the hole. Make it large enough to fit a drinking straw through.

STEP 3: Directly above this hole, make another mark 1 inch (2.5 cm) down from the top of the can.

STEP 4: Make a small hole with the scissors point at this mark.

STEP 5: Repeat steps 1-4 on the opposite side of the can, directly across from the first holes.

STEP 6: Cut 4 inches (10 cm) from the non-bending end of both the straws. Discard these pieces.

STEP 7: Stick the longer end of one straw about 1 inch (2.5 cm) into one of the bottom holes. Glue it tightly in place.

hydraulic head—pressure caused by the weight of a liquid

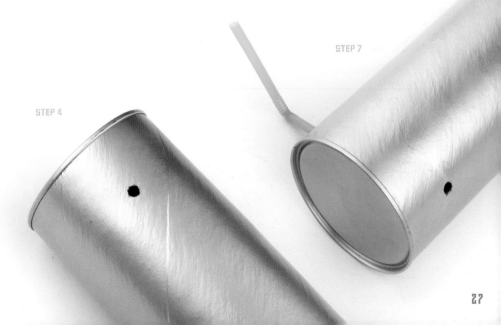

STEP 7

STEP 4

STEP 10

STEP 8: Repeat Step 7 on the opposite side.

STEP 9: Bend the straws at right angles. Make them face opposite directions.

STEP 10: Thread the string through the upper holes. Pull it even on both sides.

STEP 11: Take the engine outside, and hang it from a tree branch or hook. Allow it lots of room to move.

STEP 12: Quickly pour water into the opening of the can to fill it. Jump back if you don't want to get wet!

REUSABLE KNOWLEDGE:

Notice how much faster the engine spins when the tube is full of water. It slows as the water level drops. Water is quite heavy. Therefore the deeper water is, the more pressure it exerts. Shallow water exerts much less pressure. This phenomenon is called hydraulic head. When the hydraulic head in your engine is high, the pressure is greater. It shoots out water with a greater force, speeding up the engine. As the pressure decreases, so does the force propelling the engine.

A water tower works using a hydraulic head. Water is pumped up the tower where its weight pressurizes water pipes. The pressure pushes water out of your faucet. The tower must be higher than the houses it supplies.

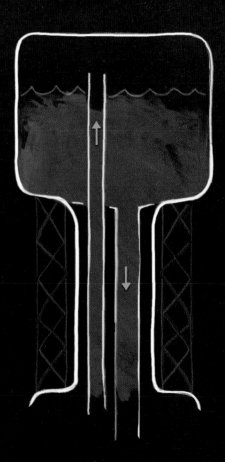

GLOSSARY

accelerate—increase speed

amplify—increase in volume

electron—particle in an atom with a negative charge

force—an action that changes the movement of an object

hydraulic head—pressure caused by the weight of a liquid

induction—charging an object by bringing it near a charged object

mass—the amount of matter a substance contains

refraction—a change in direction of a wave when it enters a different material

retina—membrane at the back of the eye

static electricity—the buildup of an electrical charge on the surface of an object

technological—the use of science to do technical things, such as designing complex machines

watt—a unit for measuring electrical power

READ MORE

Enz, Tammy. *Repurpose It: Invent New Uses for Old Stuff.* Invent It. Mankato, Minn.: Capstone Press, 2012.

Mercer, Bobby. *The Racecar Book: Build and Race Mousetrap Cars, Dragsters, Tri-can Haulers & More.* Chicago: Chicago Review Press, 2013.

Ventura, Marne. *Amazing Recycled Projects You Can Create.* Imagine It, Build It. Mankato, Minn.: Capstone Press, 2016.

INTERNET SITES

FactHound offers a safe, fun way to find Internet sites related to this book. All of the sites on FactHound have been researched by our staff.

Here's all you do:
Visit *www.facthound.com*
Type in this code: 9781515708636

Check out projects, games and lots more at
www.capstonekids.com

CRITICAL THINKING USING THE COMMON CORE

1. Explain how a pinhole camera is similar to a human eye. (Key Ideas and Details)

2. Explain what "melting point" means. (Craft and Structure)

3. Based on the explanation in the Jumping Jack project, would you expect your hair to be attracted to or repelled from the cutout after the experiment? Why? (Integration of Knowledge and Ideas)

INDEX